Reflections from the Porch

A collection of poetry and prose based on life experiences, observations, thoughts, and reflections

Written by

Anita Woodley Dennis

Edited by

Ronesha D. Dennis

Reflections from the Porch

Reflections from the Porch

Copyright © 2013 Anita W. Dennis

All rights reserved. No part of this book may be reproduced or transmitted in any format by any means without written permission from the publisher and author.

ISBN – 13:978-0615881737 (A.W. Dennis)

ISBN – 10:0615881734

Published by Anita Woodley Dennis through Createspace.com.

Edited by Ronesha D. Dennis
ronesha_dennis@yahoo.com.

Anita W. Dennis can be connected with through Facebook, Linkedin, and at adennis58@gmail.com.

Reflections from the Porch

This book is dedicated to the memory of my late parents, Fannie Hudson Woodley and Charles Joseph Woodley, Jr. It is because of the love they showed, the examples they set, and the life lessons they taught, that I am the woman I am today.

Reflections from the Porch

Contents

Acknowledgements	7
Foreword	9
Solitude	10
The Porch	12
Life and Death	14
My Life	15
The Truth	17
Life's Pathways	19
Life's Assessments	21
Life's Little Realizations	23
The Things People Do	25
Impact of Words	26
What Are You Trying to Say?	28
Life Goes On	30
Don't Weep for Me	32
Suicide Is Not an Option	34
Young Black Men Are Dying	36

Reflections from the Porch

Relationships	**38**
A Mother's Love	39
My Sole Protector	42
Daddy	43
Reunited	45
Shame	49
Friends for Life	51
True Test of Friendship	55
Forgiveness	57
Missing You	59
The Kindness of Strangers	61
Terrilynn	64
Faith and Optimism	**67**
Blessed	68
Reading Into My Soul	70
The Peace Within	71
Giving Thanks	72
Facing Adversity	73
The Power is Within You	75
Believe in Yourself	79
Let's Build Each Other Up	81

Reflections from the Porch

Keep Your Eyes on the Prize	**83**
A Brighter Tomorrow	**85**
Independence	**87**
Me Time	**88**
Caged	**90**
Take Me for Who I Am	**93**
Message to a Young Brother	**94**
Voiceless	**97**
About the Author	**101**

Acknowledgements

The motivation of family, friends, and acquaintances has been the catalyst to end my years of procrastination, and finally put thoughts to paper and write this book.

Special thanks to the following people:

My husband, Ronald Dennis, who has always encouraged me to "reach for the stars," and not let my skills and talents go to waste.

My son, Cornell, who has always inspired me to "never give up on my dreams."

My daughter, Carlette, who has been a support system - listening, analyzing, and giving constructive criticism. **Most importantly, she has not allowed me to continue procrastinating about writing this book.**

My daughter, Ronesha, who has constantly motivated me to "dig deeper in my thoughts." She is also a consummate reminder that you can achieve any goal, if you have the determination and the drive. **She also edited this book.**

My sisters: Aleta, Kathleen, Victoria, Paula, Charlene, and the late Madeline, for their love and support.

My friend, the late Viola Sykes Simmons, who taught me to never be afraid of a challenge; to see through to fruition the things that I commit to; and to follow my dreams.

Reflections from the Porch

My friend, the late Sarah Smith Rhodes, who told me more than thirty years ago that I should write a book.

My lifetime friends, Etheldra and Gwendolyn, who have always encouraged me and have **NEVER** doubted me.

My former student, Allyson Ward Neal, author, who guided and encouraged me throughout the process of writing this book.

My former student, Angela Wilson, author, who acknowledged me in her first book.

My lunchmates at O. Perry Walker College and Career Preparatory High School and Community Center. Just being in your presence and listening to you uplifted my spirit. Thank you Mrs. Stokes, Mr. and Mrs. Peters, Mrs. McQueen, Mrs. Jackson, Mrs. Charles, Mrs. Hill, Mrs. St. Amand, and Mrs. Qureshi.

My former administrators, co-workers and students at both L. B. Landry Junior-Senior High School (Aug. 1979 - Aug. 2005) and O. Perry Walker College and Career Preparatory High School and Community Center (Dec. 2005 - May 2012); thanks for the exposure and the experiences.

Thank you **all** for the inspiration, encouragement and support.

Reflections from the Porch

Foreword

Reflections from the Porch is a collection of poetry and prose that has been inspired by life experiences, observations, thoughts, and reflections.

Life experiences teach us what is right and what is wrong; they teach us what we should and should not do. They help us to face challenges, to overcome obstacles, to set goals, and to be motivated to achieve them.

Observations and thoughts open our mind to endless possibilities. They can move us in different directions, or keep us on the same positive or negative pathway.

Reflections, however, are our therapy of life. They cause us to think about our inner-self and to ask the questions: Am I all right? Can I be better? Was what I did effective? Why did I do a particular thing? Did I do the best that I possibly could? How will this make a difference? Reflections cause one to deeply examine *the self!*

Solitude

Some people equate being alone with being lonely, but for me, it's the time when I'm in my comfort zone.

This is my time to reflect about my life, its challenges, its rewards, and its journeys.

When I'm by myself, in this time of contemplation, I pray for strength, inspiration, and forgiveness.

I thank God for the blessings He has bestowed upon me.

I think about the mistakes I've made, and the positive road I want to travel in my life.

I think about the lessons I've learned and the ones I'd like to share with others.

Reflections from the Porch

Sometimes, I just walk along the levee barrier, breathing in the fresh air and looking at the muddy, but mighty, Mississippi River, watching the ships passing by, and wondering where they've been and where they're headed.

I also use this time to ponder about what I need to do to achieve my many goals—one of which is to write this book.

So, as I sit here, alone, on my front porch, in deep contemplation, the words come, and I write them down; the rhythms flow, and I add the words. As the observations make connections in my mind, I let the pages fill with my thoughts and from my imagination. Solitude can be the best time in a person's life.

Reflections from the Porch

The Porch

As I walk along the streets of my neighborhood,

I see people on the front porches of the houses I pass:

Miss Ann, sitting and talking with her elderly mom;

Mr. Joe and Miss Margie, laughing and cautiously watching their little ones playing in the front yard;

Ruth, Patricia, Almeda, and Maria, giggling and whispering about the boys they secretly admire;

Charlie and his friends, checking out the girls who stroll by;

Mr. James, smoking a cigar, appearing deep in thought;

Mr. Henry, reading the daily newspaper;

Miss Sadie, smiling and waving:

Miss Ethel, rocking her grandbaby back and forth;

Reflections from the Porch

Miss Corinne, just standing and watching the cars and the people go by;

Mr. Clarence,

Miss Virginia,

Miss Bee,

They watch;

They wave;

They laugh;

They read;

They play;

They remember;

They're deep in thought;

They reflect;

From the porch!

Life and Death

Life is filled with rewards and challenges, victories and defeats, and opportunities and setbacks. However, there is so much more to life. Life is like a story with unexpected twists and turns; it's a journey along a continuous road leading to various destinations. Throughout life, there are many lessons learned. However, at the conclusion of this journey, whether long or short, is death.

My Life

I opened my eyes to a new beginning.

I felt the warmth of a tender touch.

I heard the words of kindness and love.

I learned of the heavens in the sky above.

I smelled the fragrance of the fresh flowers.

I felt the wetness of the gentle rain.

I received the many blessings from my Savior.

I experienced joy as well as pain.

I knew passion, love, and sincerity.

I felt anger, jealousy, and rage.

I grew in knowledge, wisdom, and understanding.

I found a love that would last throughout the age.

Reflections from the Porch

My life has had many challenges

A myriad of good as well as bad,

But I wouldn't trade a day of it,

For all the gold the world has ever had.

Reflections from the Porch

The Truth

You hurt my feelings when you told me the truth.

You were blunt and honest, thinking you were doing the right thing.

But sometimes the truth isn't always what people want or need to hear.

Truth can be like blunt force trauma to the back of the skull.

Truth can be like the force of a knife being plunged into a victim's back.

Truth can be the excruciating pain one feels when hit by a speeding car.

My truth and your truth about the same situation can be totally different.

Truth can end an old friendship and begin a new one.

Truth can make one shed tears or burst into laughter.

If the truth hurts, should you tell it?

Reflections from the Porch

If a lie will save a life, but the truth will end one, what is your truth?

Can you handle the truth?

Some people can't.

The truth can end a romantic relationship.

The truth can cause self-doubt.

The truth can cause one not to be able to face and overcome challenges.

The truth can be a heavy burden on one's shoulders or the relief one feels when

that load is lifted.

The truth can be like a paradox.

While it can cause one to hate,

The truth can also cause one to love.

Reflections from the Porch

Life's Pathways

There are many roads to choose as we travel life's pathways.

Roads that take us on journeys near and far.

To places we've only dreamed about, and to those where we've been before.

Journeys where questions are asked, decisions are made, and lessons are learned;

Journeys that may lead to roadblocks and detours.

Journeys where we must climb mountains, swim oceans, and trudge down into deep, dark valleys.

As we journey, exploring these pathways, we should ask ourselves the questions,

"Is this the direction I want to travel in my life?" and "Does this road lead to a rewarding life for me?"

The final decision to choose a particular pathway is a monumental one which requires deep thought.

Reflections from the Porch

Choosing the right pathway can make all the difference in a person's life.

Reflections from the Porch

Life's Assessments

Life is full of tests!

People are tested from the time they are born until the time they die.

Throughout mothers' pregnancies, they are tested medically to ensure their own health and that of their unborn children.

Then, when those babies are born, they are tested to make sure they are healthy.

As the young children grow, they are continually assessed to make sure they are developing properly.

Before these children enter school, they must be tested to ensure their readiness.

Throughout their elementary, middle, and high school years, students will be tested to see if they are mastering concepts, or if they need remediation or extensions.

Reflections from the Porch

In order to graduate from high school, students are also required to take and pass exit exams.

Entering the military, college, or some vocations requires that people take some type of assessment.

Many college students will have to take and pass a content proficiency examination before they are allowed to graduate.

Even entering into many professional careers requires that people make a certain score on a specialized test.

And if these tests aren't enough, all of humanity, must face challenges and obstacles—tests—on a daily basis.

Yes, life is full of tests, but it is the one who is observant, who is prepared, and who has faith that will succeed.

Reflections from the Porch

Life's Little Realizations

People don't always understand you, because you don't fit "the mold"

Of the way society expects you to act, look, sound, and feel.

You often become frustrated because you can't always please people,

Especially those you love.

Some whisper about you behind your back;

Some refuse to be in your presence;

Others simply delete you from their social network.

But then you realize that you can't please everyone,

And you can't always change people's attitudes about you.

Reflections from the Porch

You also realize that their attitude towards you will not enhance your life in any way.

So, you decide to continue being yourself.

If they choose not to accept who you are,

So what!

Your life is better for it!

Less negativity!

Less anxiety!

And less stress!

Reflections from the Porch

The Things People Do

Hurtful words and evils thoughts can severely damage the priceless heart.

Whispered rumors, barely heard, can stir the pain—even when absurd.

An accidental slip of a thoughtless tongue can render the spirit lost and hung.

Careless gestures bold and obscene can leave you feeling so unclean.

Evil deeds are like a knife stab in the back – leaving you sore, breathless, and completely off track.

I can't explain; I have no clue; why people do the things we do.

We lie, cheat, curse and then—

We wish we could take it all back.

But—WE CAN'T!

… Reflections from the Porch

Impact of Words

People don't always realize how their negative words can affect others.

These words might impact their sisters, or maybe even their brothers.

The effect can spread like a wildfire, going so far that no one else can see,

That unkind words, rumors, or accusations might destroy an entire family.

So when you call someone ugly or say that they stink,

Consider their feelings and before speaking these words—think.

Be careful when passing on the words of others;

Remember to consider the source before going any further.

Research the facts and get to the truth before

making the accusation,

Reflections from the Porch

Because charges made without proof can be a source of humiliation.

So, be mindful of others' feelings before you say a word,

Because you can't take them back once your words have been heard!

Reflections from the Porch

What Are You Trying to Say?

Don't ask me that question; I believe I speak quite clear.

The words I'm saying to you; you obviously don't want to hear.

When I say your conversation is boring, I mean what you're saying is uninteresting to me.

When I say you're a bully, I mean you try to control others by telling them what to do, say, think, and feel.

When I say you're childish, I mean even though you're an adult, you act like a child.

When I say you're clumsy, I mean you're always dropping things.

When I say you're condescending, I mean you act like you're superior to others.

When I say you're gullible, I mean you allow yourself to be easily tricked.

Reflections from the Porch

When I say you're a liar, I mean you don't tell the truth.

When I say you're a pessimist, I mean you don't say anything positive.

When I say you pilfer, I mean you take things that do not belong to you.

When I say you're selfish, I mean you'll do for yourself before you even think about doing for others.

I can go on and on, being straight to the point.

But I hope you're listening so that you GET the point.

Do you know what I'm trying to say NOW?

Reflections from the Porch

Life Goes On

It's a hurtful feeling to lose someone we truly love,

Even though we know they're in Heaven with God above.

We question why they had to be taken away,

As we get down on our knees or go to a quiet place to pray.

We feel sadness, anger, hopelessness, and a sense of loss,

Knowing we would have them back in our life at any cost.

We experience a sense of numbness. It's as if we can't feel,

Yet in our mind, we know the situation is for real.

We feel that the earth should stop revolving, and time should stand still,

But we know, in our hearts, that this is God's will.

Reflections from the Porch

You see, life goes on, even when we lose someone to death.

And we must accept the fact that He knows best!

Though it's a struggle for us, we must find a way,

To get through each sleepless night and each painful day.

We shed tears of sorrow, grief, and loneliness because our loved one is gone,

But we have our cherished memories to help us move along,

And no matter how painful the ordeal –

Life goes on and time does heal!

Don't Weep for Me

When God calls me to His Heavenly home,

Don't weep for me or sing sad songs.

Raise high your voices in celebration.

Sing uplifting songs of jubilation.

When my precious Father calls for me,

Sing praise to the Lord for I'll be free.

Don't weep and mourn because I'm dead.

Just know, in your heart, I'm with Jesus instead.

When my time has come and my heart beats no more,

My soul will soar upward to Heaven's door,

And I will no longer dwell in a physical body or an earthly home.

I'll be with you in spirit though you may feel alone.

Reflections from the Porch

The toils and troubles of the world will bother me no more;

Instead, I will go to be with My Father, the One I adore.

Reflections from the Porch

Suicide Is Not an Option

If those dark thoughts swirl through your head,

That sometimes you wish that you were dead,

Think carefully, and take this advice:

Keep a positive outlook on life.

Of course you'll miss someone you loved and lost.

But cherish the precious memories, at any cost.

We all make them for heaven's sake,

So please own up to your mistakes.

When you do wrong, even under duress,

Always ask for His forgiveness.

If, in Him, you truly believe,

Be thankful for everything you have received.

Seek help with your mental healing,

By talking to someone about your feelings.

Don't think of it selfishly,

Reflections from the Porch

Just love yourself unconditionally.

Don't act on impulse; it isn't right;

Fight those feelings with all your might.

So before taking drastic measures, think twice,

Don't give up on yourself and on life.

Enjoy living; it's what you were put on Earth to do.

Life is a journey; don't miss out; just see it through.

Look optimistically toward your future goals;

Say, "I CAN DO IT!" as you travel along life's road.

Reflections from the Porch

Young Black Men Are Dying

Young Black men are dying everyday

Because they think gun violence is the only way.

Shooting each other with deadly force,

They have no regrets and show no remorse.

Young Black men are dying everyday

Because they think that selling drugs will give them pay.

Making a quick dollar to live a good life

Which ends up being shortened by a gun or knife.

Young Black men are dying everyday

Because they think their manhood was threatened in some way.

Some leaving innocent children without a dad

Reflections from the Porch

And their families left feeling anger and despair.

Young Black men are dying everyday

Because they think they own the neighborhoods where they stay.

Fighting to protect an address or a street

Which doesn't care if they win or feel defeat.

Yes, young Black men are dying everywhere,

Becoming statistics in a world in desperate need of repair.

Relationships

Relationships shape who we become in life. Whether it's to guide us in a positive direction or a negative one, these connections impact our lives. We acquire wisdom and knowledge from them and aspire to reach our goals because of them. These links teach us to love ourselves and others. Observations and interactions influence our thoughts, words, and actions.

Reflections from the Porch

A Mother's Love

She held our hands when we were young,

Leading us, guiding us, and protecting us from harm.

She listened to our comments, complaints and concerns,

Even when she was too busy or too tired to respond.

She assisted us with homework and monitored our progress in school,

Even when she really didn't understand all of the assignments.

Mother bought our clothes, food, school supplies, and gifts,

Even when bills were due and money was extremely limited.

Reflections from the Porch

She encouraged us to always pay attention, to listen for understanding, and to practice for reinforcement.

Mother always told us to believe in ourselves and to love ourselves.

She said to never be afraid of a challenge because life was full of them.

She said that we should surround ourselves with smart, positive, "action" people because that kind of behavior was a great influence.

Mother led by example, being humble, kind, generous, respectful, and courteous.

She also always said, "please" when asking, and "thank you" for anything she received.

But most importantly, mother always said, "The Lord is my shepherd; I shall not want," and "Trust in the Lord; He'll make a way."

Reflections from the Porch

She was a prime example of what a mother should be!

Reflections from the Porch

My Sole Protector

When you wrap your arms around me,

I feel so safe and warm.

You are my sole protector.

You keep me safe from harm.

When you whisper soft words to me,

They're what I want to hear.

You are my sole protector.

You keep me safe and near.

When you hold my hand so gently,

Please don't let it go.

You are my sole protector.

That's why I love you so.

Reflections from the Porch

Daddy

A hard man to love, but we had no choice.

You WERE our daddy.

You were there when we needed you most.

Your powerful, booming voice only gave a command once.

Your cool, dark brown, piercing eyes could see straight through us.

You gave the answers before the questions were asked.

You provided as best you could, even when we wanted more than you could afford to give.

You tried your best to protect us girls from the cruel world.

But we all had to experience it for ourselves.

You also had a soft side that you let out from time to time.

Reflections from the Porch

You showed compassion for others, pride in our accomplishments, and a strong faith in God.

You said, "Give me my flowers while I can still smell them!"

And I hope we did!

You ARE and will forever be our daddy!

Reflections from the Porch

Reunited

She abandoned you and your sister, and ran off with her man.

He didn't want to be bothered with the two of you; you didn't fit into his plan.

He considered children a hindrance, a bother, and a pain.

And he told your mom, if she didn't leave the two of you, she'd never see him again.

Tears flowed from your eyes, and your sister cried, of course,

But when you looked into your mother's eyes, they showed no sign of remorse.

You were three at the time, and your big sister was only ten.

There were no other relatives; you two had no clue where to begin.

Reflections from the Porch

You tried to take care of each other, but that plan soon came to an end,

When a nosey, but caring neighbor called the authorities, who immediately stepped in.

Soon after, you two were separated, not knowing what would be your fate.

You both were now placed into foster care, becoming wards of the state.

Anger, bitterness, and distrust fueled your thoughts and actions;

To any kindness offered, you had a negative reaction.

Years passed with no contact between you two - sister and brother,

And you no longer cared about the whereabouts of your mother.

She had left you to fend for yourselves without thought or care,

Reflections from the Porch

Of what would be your fate without her presence there.

Eventually, your older sister, who loved you with all her heart,

Was able to find and get custody of you, without a second thought.

She had become of age, and through research and a lot of prayer,

Found you, and took you into her care.

By now, the anger and bitterness were so deep inside of you,

It was hard to find the serenity that calms the spirit so true.

But some of that misery subsided, because your sister was back in your life,

And you found that peace, that inner strength, to put aside the turmoil and the strife.

Reflections from the Porch

Now, you thank God daily for her perseverance, tenacity, and love,

And that He provided her with the direction and the guidance from above.

Even though you two were abandoned, and felt a sense of hopelessness and pain,

It was through His divine intervention that you two found each other again.

Reflections from the Porch

Shame

I cry for my mom and our family every night,

Because we are living a life filled with turmoil and strife.

My father, who abandoned the family, is addicted to both alcohol and crack cocaine.

It's a wonder our household isn't totally insane.

We live in the ghetto, surrounded by violent crimes and gunfire.

Living a life safe from harm is our only desire.

The tears that I cry roll down like the blood that so many have shed.

Each day our lives are filled with fear and dread.

Nobody knows or even suspects,

The shame we children feel, being victims of neglect.

Reflections from the Porch

My mother tries her best to support her five kids.

And we do appreciate the hard work, effort, and love that she gives.

But she works three jobs, which leaves us alone.

Until recently, we had no adult supervision because she was always gone.

But, it is only by grace and the power of prayer

That our elderly grandmother has stepped in to show us some care.

We have moved into her home, so we won't be alone,

And in her neighborhood, we feel safe from harm.

The shame that we once felt is with us no more.

The shame that we once felt has gone, to return, hopefully, NEVERMORE.

Reflections from the Porch

Friends for Life

You are my friend for life!

When we first met in kindergarten, we gravitated to each other instantly.

We giggled, ran around, whispered secrets, and kept each other company.

That bond continued throughout high school and college.

Even as adults, living in different states, we are still connected to each other.

You are my friend for life!

When we first met in sixth grade, I was new to the school and to the neighborhood.

You befriended me when others alienated me.

We visited each other's homes, went on adventures, laughed, cried, and discussed our feelings about boys.

Reflections from the Porch

Our special bond continues to this day.

You are my friend for life!

When we met on the job, we quickly became like sisters.

We confided in each other, discussed professional issues, shopped, and experienced different cuisines together.

Even though you are no longer here, I feel the connection of our souls.

You are my friend for life!

You are also my sister.

I have always known you, and I have always loved you.

We pray together, travel together, and confide in each other.

As we grow older and wiser, we realize that no one can break the bond we share.

Reflections from the Porch

You are my friends for life!

You are also my children.

We keep each other company.

We tell each other the truth, even when it hurts.

We call and text each other just to keep in touch.

We tell each other, "I love you!"

You are my friend for life!

You are also my husband.

We have shared many wonderful experiences.

We have seen each other through difficult times.

We have been angry with each other, and forgiven each other.

We don't always say it, but we know we love each other.

True friends are like precious gems!

They are valuable and rare.

Reflections from the Porch

They will support and uplift you.

They will pray for your well-being and success.

They will always love you, unconditionally!

Reflections from the Porch

True Test of Friendship

I made a mistake, and it hurt your feelings and made you cry,

But I didn't have the words to say "I'm sorry," or try to explain my reason why.

We were friends, and I should have honored your trust.

There is no excuse for betraying a confidence, which lays the grounds for mistrust.

I began to avoid you, not daring to confront you face to face.

I asked God to forgive me; I asked for His grace.

But I should have also asked for your forgiveness, as I am doing right now.

Please accept my apology; I was wrong; please let us go on as friends somehow.

For in all my life, I have never found a wonderful friend like you;

Reflections from the Porch

Someone to have fun with and to tell all my troubles to.

It is so unfortunate that you tried to do the same,

But I was too immature to understand that friendship is not to be played like a game.

It is a bond, a strong adhesive; it's tight like superglue,

And with true friendship there is forgiveness and understanding which is what I have with you.

You accepted my apology more quickly than I ever would have thought, and

It was evident that your acceptance was sincerely from your heart.

You allayed my doubts and fears, and put my mind at ease

You showed me that the true test of friendship is one that can withstand

challenges, setbacks, and last through anything!

Forgiveness

You call yourself my friend, but you did something a friend would never do.

But because I am a Christian, I know in my heart I must forgive you.

It was a painful experience to feel that knife stabbed so deeply into my back,

Knowing it was done by someone I had known so far back,

Back when we were young, adventurous and care free,

Back when we had each other's backs --- I could guarantee.

What you did hurt so badly, I didn't know what to do.

Reflections from the Porch

But because I am a strong person, I knew in my heart I must forgive you.

We shared profound secrets; things we swore to never tell,

But on the day you betrayed my trust, I thought to myself, "You can go straight to hell!"

Forgiveness, for you, was difficult for me to find.

But that Greater Power, that Force that we all know,

Told me to dig deep in my heart to forgive you, AND JUST LET GO!

AND because I have a strong faith in God, and He has forgiven me,

I had to find, not only the strength, but also the courage to forgive you,

To allow MYSELF to be free.

Reflections from the Porch

Missing You

Never thought I'd miss you so;

Never thought I'd feel this way;

But in my heart I knew that you'd leave someday.

Why did we have to part?

Why did you say goodbye?

I guess everything you said to me was really just a lie.

You've left me feeling so confused;

It makes me think I've been abused;

I only hope as time goes by,

That I won't stop to cry.

Missing you – can't stop the pain.

I feel like I'm walking in the rain.

Reflections from the Porch

Don't tell me not to feel this way,

Just come back into my life to stay.

I can't take anymore of this;

It's your love I truly miss.

I don't want love from no one else,

I just want you for myself.

You've left me in such misery,

When all I want is ecstasy.

Missing you – can't stop the pain.

I feel like I'm running through the rain.

Don't tell me not to feel this way,

Just come back into my life to stay.

Reflections from the Porch

The Kindness of Strangers

(Dedicated to those, all over this nation, who unselfishly assisted the victims of Hurricanes Katrina and Rita in 2005)

With warmth in their opened arms,

And politeness in their uplifted voices,

They welcomed us strangers into their states, cities, and homes.

Feeling our pain, hopelessness, and loss from the hurricanes' devastation,

They mouthed heartfelt, inspirational words of motivation.

The kindness of strangers will never be forgotten.

With sincerity in their eyes,

And graciousness in their deeds,

Reflections from the Porch

They offered generous support and fulfilled our daily needs.

Backing their words with actions was their creed.

For every request for help, there was a kind reaction,

Which left us "refugees" with a feeling of satisfaction.

For never in our lives could we have imagined,

That we would have found ourselves in this place,

Of fear, despair, and downright disgrace.

But it was the kindness of strangers that brought us through.

They encouraged and motivated us to know what to do.

They filled our hearts with pride and humility.

They gave us a strong feeling of sensibility.

Reflections from the Porch

They made us realize that tragedies happen, and God will see us through.

And that the next kindness from a stranger can easily come from within me or you.

Reflections from the Porch

Terrilynn

(Dedicated to Terrilynn Monette – Jefferson Parish elementary school teacher who went missing on March 2, 2013)

Where are you, our sweet angel?

We miss you so very much!

We have looked every place we could think of,

Searching from dawn until dusk.

Your disappearance is such a mystery,

And it's been too long since you've been gone.

Our lives are devastated, and we feel so forlorn,

But what hurts more than anything is that we have no clue;

We haven't heard a word or seen any sign of you.

You are such a pretty girl, innocent and pure;

Only twenty – six years old,

Reflections from the Porch

Your career was just beginning; you were just starting to soar.

But we don't know where you are,

And it saddens us to our heart's core.

We've searched parks, woods, and bayous and knocked on every door.

Baffled family, friends, and strangers, have increased the reward,

Pleading for information on your whereabouts and your missing Honda Accord.

 We refuse to believe that we will not hear from or see you anymore!

But on June 8th your car was found

When a volunteer Slidell police officer dove down,

Down into an unsearched area of Bayou St. John;

To our devastation, your body was finally found

Reflections from the Porch

And it was the coroner's determination that you had drowned.

But it was the persistence of your family and La. State Representative Austin Badon,

That this heart wrenching search had continued on,

For ninety – eight days without cease.

Hoping to bring some closure to family and friends in grief.

This agonizing search has now come to an end,

And you, Terrilynn, can now rest in peace!

(Terrilynn's body was found inside of her car in Bayou St. John on June 8, 2013. The New Orleans coroner determined that Terrilynn Monette had drowned.)

Reflections from the Porch

Faith and Optimism

People can accomplish anything they set their minds to, if they have faith in God and themselves, and confidence and determination. There will be setbacks and challenges that will sometimes seem difficult to overcome, but perseverance, courage, and effort will ultimately lead to victory.

Reflections from the Porch

Blessed

He awakens me each morning to fulfill the promises of a new day.

He listens to my words and knows my thoughts as I get down on my knees to pray.

He inspires me to be a productive force in others' lives.

He motivates me to complete every goal to which I strive.

He protects me and keeps me safe from harm.

He forgives me when I repent for the things I think, say, or do wrong.

He gives me courage, strength, and faith.

He is my Savior,

And my saving grace.

He wraps His arms around me each and every day,

Reflections from the Porch

He sustains me on the arduous journey along my way,

He guides me along each path I choose, to reach whatever my goal may be.

He keeps me strong when I face personal losses, or when my life is filled with grief.

He understands me, even when I don't understand myself.

He gives me commonsense to know, when in trouble, I should ask for His help.

He provides me with faith that is undeniably strong.

He loves me even when I do things that are wrong.

I feel His presence and His loving care, and I know in my heart He is always there.

I am blessed, and I have no doubts.

I am blessed; let the world hear me shout!

Reflections from the Porch

Reading into My Soul

Deep within are my inner thoughts
That keep me safe and far apart
From the eyes and ears that seek and spy
To know the secrets that are deep inside.

My inner thoughts are there for me;
They contain my inner mystery.
Many try to seek and spy,
Searching to find the pain inside.

No one knows my inner thoughts, you see;
They're hidden deep inside of me.
The struggles I've endured and the triumphs, too.
The love we've shared between us two.

The mirror of my soul reflects the true me:
I know what others cannot see.
I know what others cannot tell.
If you could read my soul, you'd know as well.

Reflections from the Porch

The Peace Within

There is an inner peace that dwells within us all;

That comforts us throughout the night and well into the dawn,

That tempers our heated anger and renders a lasting calm,

That soothes our haunting fears and keeps us safe from harm.

The peace within that strengthens us and helps us to feel free,

Provides a lasting sense of deep serenity.

Reflections from the Porch

Giving Thanks

I thank Him for everything He has done for me –

To awake me each day, so that I may start anew,

To bless me with a family to love and cherish me, so true,

To lead and guide me through challenges and tests,

To uplift my spirits when I feel down, so that I can be motivated to do my very best,

To answer my prayers and give me strength,

To give me courage and stand by my side in my defense;

I thank God for all the blessings He has bestowed on me,

And Heavenly Father, I offer my constant faith and everlasting love to Thee!

Facing Adversity

I was afraid of you because you hurt me.

I cried when you undressed me;

I closed my eyes when you touched me;

I screamed when you forced yourself on me.

"No, don't do that!"

"Leave me alone!"

"It hurts so bad!"

"I'm gonna tell my mama!"

But in spite of my protests,

You touched me!

You hurt me!

You made me ache in excruciating pain!

Reflections from the Porch

You told me if I said a word about this, I'd never see my mama again!

I continued to suffer, enduring humiliation, mental and physical pain.

But words from my mother echoed in my ears over and over again.

"Have faith in God; He will see you through.

He is forever there, standing right next to you."

She said, "I love you, and God loves you too.

Count on us; we'll know what to do."

So I finally told my mother, and now you are in jail.

A jury found you guilty, and justice did prevail.

No other little girl will suffer from your cruelty and hate;

Life imprisonment was the sentence; it sealed your fate.

Reflections from the Porch

The Power is Within You

Life is full of lessons! And as we go through life, we also realize that we must overcome setbacks and challenges that are designed to interfere with us fulfilling our goals and desires. It is very easy to miss an opportunity, misinterpret, misunderstand, or simply miss wise instructions or observations, by not being focused or paying attention.

It is the wise person who soon realizes that the power to accomplish anything begins within him or her. Murphy's Law says that "if something can go wrong, it will go wrong." In life, we may have well-intentioned plans, but those plans may not pan out like we had hoped. In spite of setbacks, however, we must not lose faith or abandon our dreams. We must not simply accept defeat because things didn't go as planned. We must look within ourselves to find that drive, that push, that motivation to inspire us to not give up and to move forward. Sometimes, we simply have to change directions or find another way to achieve our goals and fulfill our dreams.

Reflections from the Porch

But we must first:

- Believe in ourselves. If we don't believe in ourselves, how can we expect anyone else to believe in us? When we believe in ourselves, we can overcome any difficulties, challenges, or obstacles in our paths.

We must also have:

- **Love and respect.** "The greatest achievement for any human being is to love; to love God, to love and respect others, but most importantly to love and respect yourself."

We can't feel that sense of satisfaction and accomplishment if we don't:

- Set goals for ourselves: **Set long term and short term goals.** Decide what it is we want to achieve today, next week, within the next month, within a year, within the next five years. What are our dreams? In order to accomplish something, we have to make a plan or have some idea of what it is that we want to achieve.

Reflections from the Porch

Remember, however, along the way, we will have to:

- Overcome obstacles. Life is full of obstacles, roadblocks, and challenges. Through determination, perseverance, hard work and effort, we will succeed.

Also, along our journey to achieving our goals, we may get hurt; someone may do us wrong, or WE may do someone harm. That's why forgiveness is important.

- Forgiveness: We must forgive ourselves for our wrongs and transgressions, and forgive others for theirs. This is not easy, and it may take some time, but the feeling of peace in knowing that we have been forgiven or that we have forgiven someone else is rewarding.

We can't go wrong if we:

- Surround ourselves with positivity. The people around us have a tendency to influence our thoughts and behavior. If we are constantly in an environment of negativity, it will surely rub off on us. Vice versa, if we surround ourselves with positive thinking and acting people, it will certainly influence our thoughts and actions.

Finally, and most importantly:

- Faith: Having a strong belief in a higher power, such as God, is paramount. That faith will keep us on a steady and positive course to being the best people we can be.

Believe in Yourself

When you believe in yourself, you feel good about yourself.

When you have that inner pride, you don't put yourself down.

When you don't put yourself down, you uplift yourself.

When you uplift yourself, you treat yourself like you're a king or a queen.

When you treat yourself like royalty, you're in control.

When you're in control, you have a positive outlook on life.

When you have a positive outlook on life, you see the good in others.

When you see the good in others, you treat them with respect.

When you treat others with respect, they see the respect you have for yourself,

Reflections from the Porch

and you get the same in return.

And when you have that feeling of self-love and respect, that uplifting spirit, you not only have a positive outlook on life, but also, you're motivated to know that the sky is the limit, and nothing will stand in your way.

Your tenacity and perseverance make you know that you can overcome any challenges, adversities, or obstacles you might face on your road to achieving your personal success!

Reflections from the Porch

Let's Build Each Other Up

We're so busy tearing each other down when we should be building each other up. Rather than "hating" on our fellow man, we should be busy instilling trust. Trust that he will succeed and pave the way for others, reaching back to lend a helping hand to a "sister" or "brother".

It's so sad to hear people putting each other down when we should be lending that helping hand. Rather than talking about someone behind their back, we should be remembering that this is our fellow man. So, in support of him, we should be doing all that we can.

This is the perfect time to encourage, motivate, and show praise for one's ability to succeed; rather than showing jealousy, spite, envy, or even greed.

Envy, because we didn't take the initiative or have the drive, to strive for our dreams, pushing all obstacles aside.

Reflections from the Porch

Spite, because we were afraid to take the chance, to attempt to achieve our goal, overcoming any challenging circumstance.

Envy, because we didn't have the confidence to stick with "it," so we just decided to give it all up and just quit.

Greed, because we felt a little bad; we just weren't willing to do the work to get something that someone else had.

So rather than put someone down, let's build each other up; think about the joy you feel when you're being lifted up.

It's such a good feeling when we've achieved a goal, and someone gives us accolades; it like a blessing of our soul.

And it's that same blessing that will come back to you, because when you build someone else up, you're really building yourself up, too.

Reflections from the Porch

Keep Your Eyes on the Prize

Stay focused and believe that you can achieve what you set your mind to do.

Set goals for yourself and do everything possible to see them through.

Don't let challenges and adversities stand in your way.

Just concentrate on the outcome and the objectives to be achieved one day.

Those who love you will support you; they will forever be by your side.

They will encourage you in your endeavors, while showing their heartfelt pride.

Sometimes peers will try to influence you to travel a negative road.

Reflections from the Porch

But keep your eyes on the prize, even when burdened with a heavy load.

It does not matter your economic status: whether born into wealth or poverty.

Believe in yourself, work hard, and never give up, as you journey to victory.

A Brighter Tomorrow

You can't deny it because you know it's true.

You took the best of me; I gave my all to you.

Now I sit here empty, bewildered, and blue,

Longing for something to make me feel worthy of YOU.

I think to myself, what a pitiful, depressing state!

Is this my destiny, my reward, my fate?

Is this what I've allowed myself to become,

Bitter, angry, lost, and just plain numb?

Snap out of it; get over them; move on with your life!

There's a brighter rainbow on the horizon,

A beacon of hope, an enduring light.

Reflections from the Porch

Unwavering and shining, filling the sky so blue.

Ending a chapter in your life, so that you can start anew.

Reflections from the Porch

Independence

I'm an independent person and I think for myself;

I don't rely on the decisions of anyone else.

I set my goals high and THEM, I work hard to achieve;

I'm not afraid of a challenge because, in myself, I truly believe.

I make my own rules, and I don't follow the crowd;

I'm hardworking, honest, focused, and proud.

I'm intrinsically motivated with high self-esteem;

With faith in God and myself, I know I will achieve any dream.

Me Time

I need some "me" time –

A little quality time

Just to be free time

And reflect on me.

I need some "I" time –

Just a little my time

Even if I want to cry time

To release the stress in me.

I need some "lone" time –

Just to be on my own time

Even if I want to sing a song time

Without company.

Reflections from the Porch

I need some "reflect" time –

Just to resurrect time

Just to self-assess time

And allow myself to feel free.

Caged

Sometimes I feel trapped like a bird in a cage,

Unable to fly unencumbered through the air,

Flapping my wings without a care,

Soaring through the sky, flying ever so high,

Chirping freedom's song all day long.

Sometimes I feel confined like a prisoner in a cell,

Unable to unleash my inner rage,

Not able to say what I want to say,

Or be who I want to be,

Not able to reveal my inner mystery.

Sometimes I feel restricted, cramped in a limited place;

I want to move about freely,

Reflections from the Porch

But I'm confined to this tiny space.

The walls seem to move in on me;

I push them back with all my strength.

Sometimes I feel cornered, struggling to break free.

The secrets kept hidden deep inside of me;

No one knows my emotional pain;

I'm under so much stress; it's like I'm slowly going insane.

I long for the day when I can sing freedom's song;

The day when the mountains will be moved,

And the valleys will be gone.

I will swim across the ocean;

I will soar across the sky.

There will be no more evil, only peace and love will abide;

Reflections from the Porch

My confinement will be over, and I will be at peace!

Reflections from the Porch

Take Me for Who I Am

Don't analyze me.

Don't belittle me.

Don't challenge me.

Don't be condescending towards me.

Don't dismiss me.

Don't disrespect me.

Don't harass me.

Don't judge me.

Don't offend me.

Don't patronize me.

Don't put me down.

Don't question me.

Don't ridicule me.

Don't try to change me.

JUST LET ME BE WHO I AM!

Reflections from the Porch

Message to a Young Brother

Hey young brother, stand proud and tall!

Don't hang your head down or let your shoulders fall.

You've had some difficult struggles, and life for you has not been kind.

But don't let the mountains and valleys, the burdens and the heavy loads,

Make you angry, cause you to have self-doubt or explode.

You've had some dark days when your skies were overcast;

You couldn't find the courage and the fortitude to let them pass;

The road ahead appeared dismal and dim,

And it seemed you'd lost all faith in Him.

Your mother died from cancer;

Your father was nowhere around;

Reflections from the Porch

Your older brother succumbed to drugs;

Your sister struggles as a single, teenaged mom;

Your younger brother was shot and killed right in front of you.

You feel so hopeless, not knowing what to do.

You think your life is pointless; there's nowhere forward to move.

You've decided to end your life; you just can't go on.

But I say to you young brother – just hold on. Be strong!

Life is not easy; it's like a bumpy road.

It's full of roadblocks and detours and changing directions.

It's like that street that you travel that's full of imperfections.

And like that bumpy road, that turns and goes many ways

You have to look within yourself; search deep inside,

Reflections from the Porch

To find the stamina, the fortitude, and even the pride,

To realize negative things happen, and it's not your fault

To surround yourself with positive people, so you won't feel alone

To set goals for your future and work hard to fulfill your dreams

And, to love yourself, even when you think no one else will.

Voiceless

Who's going to speak for the baby, born into poverty?

A child brought into the world without the basic necessities,

Born into a place where the essentials of life have been denied,

And it's a major struggle for him to even survive.

Who's going to speak for the little boy who's being abused in his own home?

It certainly won't be his mother because she leaves him all alone.

She locks him in a tiny closet and goes out to party all night.

She knows that this is wrong, but she figures he'll be all right.

Reflections from the Porch

Who's going to speak for the little fellow who witnessed his father's death?

He watched his dad being murdered by men who showed no remorse and had no regrets.

This young man struggles, consumed by nightmares and fear;

He thinks they will come back to murder him because they live so near.

Who's going to speak for the little girl who's experiencing both physical and mental pain?

Her own father keeps raping her over and over again.

She can't tell her mother for fear of HER demise.

So this precious child suffers with her voiceless, silent cries.

Who's going to speak for the little children being beaten by mama's boyfriend?

Reflections from the Porch

Mama certainly won't stop him because she doesn't want their relationship to end.

So they ALL suffer in silence as the abuse goes on and on,

No one able to stop it because they have no voice of their own.

I hear the cries of the impoverished.

I hear the pounding of the trapped and neglected.

I hear the screams of the physically, sexually, and emotionally abused.

I hear the pleas of these fearful victims, suffering and mute.

Do you hear them?

So, will you speak for them?

Who will speak for the innocent victims who cannot speak for themselves?

Reflections from the Porch

We, who have the platforms,

We, who have the courage,

We, who have the power,

We, who have the strength,

Most importantly, we, who have the conviction,

Must use our voices to advocate for those who suffer in silence.

Reflections from the Porch

About the Author

Anita Woodley Dennis is a retired educator who is a native of New Orleans, Louisiana. She holds a Bachelor of Arts Degree in English Education from Southern University at New Orleans and a Master of Education in Curriculum and Instruction from The University of New Orleans. Anita is also a certified reading specialist. She taught high school English for 33 years. Anita often encouraged her students to write original poetry and to read the poetry of noted authors because she feels that poetry is inspirational, motivational, and therapeutic. **Reflections from the Porch** was inspired by life.

Anita is married to Ronald Dennis and is the proud mother of Cornell D. Woodley and Carlette and Ronesha Dennis. She is the loving mother-in-law of April Woodley and the devoted grandmother of Derek, Symbria, and Cydne.

Reflections from the Porch

Anita enjoys reading, writing poetry, and public speaking. She is currently writing her next book, ***Writing an Effective Educational Grant Proposal***.

www.ingramcontent.com/pod-product-compliance
Lightning Source LLC
Chambersburg PA
CBHW071154090426
42736CB00012B/2325